CLASS 31 LOCOMOTIVES

Andrew Cole

AMBERLEY

First published 2016

Amberley Publishing
The Hill, Stroud
Gloucestershire, GL5 4EP

www.amberley-books.com

Copyright © Andrew Cole, 2016

The right of Andrew Cole to be identified as
the Author of this work has been asserted in
accordance with the Copyrights, Designs and
Patents Act 1988.

ISBN 978 1 4456 5791 2 (print)
ISBN 978 1 4456 5792 9 (ebook)

British Library Cataloguing in Publication Data.
A catalogue record for this book is available from
the British Library.

Typesetting by Amberley Publishing.
Printed in the UK.

Introduction

The Class 31 story started in the 1950s. Brush Traction at Loughborough constructed twenty diesel-electric locomotives in 1957 for Eastern Region passenger workings. These were known as Brush Type 2s and these twenty locomotives were to remain non-standard to the other members of the class and were originally classified as Class 30s. Over the next five years another 243 locomotives were built, again at Loughborough.

Originally the locomotives were built with Mirrlees JVS12T engines, but these were to prove unsuccessful, and a fleet-wide replacement was implemented, this being the English Electric 12SVT engine.

In 1974 British Rail introduced the TOPS renumbering scheme, and the original twenty locomotives were renumbered into the 31/0 series, from 31001 to 31019, with one example becoming 31101. The production members were then renumbered in the 31/1 number range from 31102 to 31327. The remaining seventeen locomotives were fitted with ETH equipment and were renumbered into the 31/4 number series, from 31401 to 31417.

The Class 31s had an unusual feature, the bogies being A1A-A1A, the only locos to be built as such. The fleet would remain relatively intact until the 1980s when withdrawals started, mainly through collision damage and a downturn in traffic.

The locos retained their BR blue livery until 1985, when the Railfreight grey livery started to appear. This led to an explosion of different liveries on the class, ranging from red-stripe Railfreight, triple-grey Railfreight, through to Regional Railways livery.

Over time another batch of 31s was fitted with ETH equipment, bringing the number of 31/4 locos up to seventy, being numbered 31400 to 31469. A number of these locos were to have their ETH equipment isolated, and they were renumbered into the 31/5 series for use on Civil Engineers workings.

Wholesale withdrawals continued through the 1990s, by which time the vast majority had been withdrawn and sent to the scrapyard. The main scrappers being M. C. Metals Springburn, C. F. Booth Rotherham and T. J. Thomson, Stockton.

Quite a large number were to be preserved at various locations throughout the country, however seven of the preserved locos have since found their way to the scrapyard. There are a handful still in use on the main line today working for small operators on a spot hire basis, and Network Rail have recently retired their remaining 31s.

This book is not meant to be an in-depth technical overview of the class, more of a personal recollection of a favourite class of locos. Most of the photographs were taken on the Midland Region, with some taken a bit further afield.

I hope you enjoy looking through this album, and hopefully it will jog some distant memories, or if you are new to the hobby, it may give you a flavour of a workhorse of the BR diesel era.

No. 31006, 13 April 1980

No. 31006 (D5506) is seen at Stratford TMD, East London, having been withdrawn three months earlier. This loco was built in 1958, and was part of the original batch of Class 31s. It would later be moved to Doncaster Works for scrapping, this being completed in December 1980.

No. 31015, 27 July 1980

No. 31015 (D5515) is another of the original batch of Class 31s built by Brush, Loughborough, in the late 1950s. 31015 emerged in 1958 and went straight to the Eastern Region. It was renumbered from D5515 in 1974, and is seen at Doncaster Works having been withdrawn two months earlier. It would only last another four months, being cut up in November 1980.

No. 31101, 3 November 1992

No. 31101 (D5518) is seen at Washwood Heath, Birmingham, with a train of newly made sleepers from the nearby RMC facility. No. 31101 carries a unique livery applied by its home depot at the time, Bescot.

No. 31101, 11 June 2006

No. 31101 (D5518) is seen preserved at the Battlefield Line, near Market Bosworth.

No. 31102, 2 July 1996

No. 31102 (D5520) is seen at a busy Washwood Heath with a train of newly made sleepers, coupled with No. 31554. No. 31102 carries the name *Cricklewood*, and also has been fitted with a headlight under the driver's window. No. 31102 would eventually be sold to Harry Needle and was stored at Carnforth. It was then sold onto Network Rail for spares, before being broken up by European Metal Recycling, Kingsbury, in April 2007.

No. 31105, 27 August 1995

No. 31105 (D5523) is seen on display at the Basford Hall open day, Crewe, in its unique two-tone grey livery, but with a Transrail logo. No. 31105 was named *Bescot & Saltley Quality Assured*, but in this view the 'Saltley' part has been ground down. No. 31105 would go on to see further use with Network Rail.

No. 31105, 5 August 1996

No. 31105 (D5523) is seen at Washwood Heath in two-tone grey livery with Transrail's logo, along with No. 31439, which carries Regional Railways livery. No. 31105 was named *Bescot & Saltley Quality Approved*.

No. 31105, 18 April 1987

No. 31105 (D5523) is seen at Tyseley depot, Birmingham awaiting repairs, surrounded by first-generation DMUs.

No. 31105, 27 July 1980
No. 31105 (D5523) stands on accommodation bogies at Doncaster Works, while its own bogies are off for repair.

No. 31107, 5 July 1985
No. 31107 (D5525) departs Lawley Street Freightliner Terminal with a rake of empty wagons.

No. 31107, 17 May 1991

No. 31107 (D5525) runs through Olton station with a rake of engineers' wagons. No. 31107 carries Civil Engineers livery, which was also known as 'Dutch' livery.

No. 31107, 30 August 1992

No. 31107 (D5525) stands at Bescot during the open day in 1992 when it received the name *John H. Carless V.C.* No. 31107 would go on to be used in a Network Rail level crossing awareness campaign before being scrapped by Ron Hull Junior, Rotherham, in May 2009.

No. 31108, 14 August 1982

No. 31108 (D5526) is seen having arrived at Birmingham New Street with a passenger working. No. 31108 was preserved by the A1A group, Butterley.

No. 31108, 23 May 2009

No. 31108 (D5526) is seen on display at Eastleigh Works open day in 2009, having been preserved, and looks good in original Railfreight livery complete with snow ploughs.

No. 31112, 1 June 1996

No. 31112 (D5530) passes through Crewe station in Civil Engineers 'Dutch' livery complete with Transrail logo. This was the only Class 31 to carry this livery, and would be scrapped in 2003 by T. J. Thomson, Stockton.

No. 31112, 27 February 1988

No. 31112 (D5530) carries red-stripe Railfreight livery while awaiting repairs at Tyseley depot, Birmingham. I feel this livery sat nicely on the Class 31s.

No. 31116, 12 July 1992

No. 31116 (D5534) is seen on display at Doncaster Works open day in Civil Engineers 'Dutch' livery. No. 31116 carries the name *Rail 1981–1991*.

No. 31116, 27 May 1996

No. 31116 (D5534) stands stored at Toton yard carrying its unique Infrastructure livery. This was the only Class 31 to carry this livery, and would be sent north to T. J. Thomson, Stockton, for scrapping.

No. 31117, 3 September 1986

No. 31117 (D5535) awaits its next duty at Saltley depot, Birmingham. This loco was involved in a collision the following month, and was taken to Doncaster Works for repairs, which were not forthcoming, and was eventually scrapped at Doncaster in September 1988.

No. 31119, 1 May 1985

No. 31119 (D5537) departs Lawley Street Freightliner Terminal, Birmingham, with a container working. This loco was preserved at the Embsay & Bolton Abbey Railway.

No. 31121, 14 November 1984

No. 31121 (D5539) sits at Saltley depot, Birmingham, in between turns. This skinhead Class 31 is different in that it doesn't have the foot holes in the centre panel. This Class 31 would be withdrawn in 1988 and taken to M. C. Metals, Springburn, for cutting, which took place in September 1990.

No. 31123, 20 September 1986

No. 31123 (D5541) stands inside Tyseley on the depot's wheel lathe. This loco was initially preserved, based on the Gloucestershire & Warwickshire Railway, but would end up being sold to A1A locos and would be scrapped by C. F. Booth's in February 2006.

No. 31124, 21 December 1983

No. 31124 (D5542) is seen stabled at Saltley depot, Birmingham, in BR blue livery along with classmate No. 31200. At this time there was not much deviation from the BR blue livery, however the advent of Railfreight grey was to change all that with the introduction of the Class 58s.

No. 31126, 1 September 1987

No. 31126 (D5544) arrives at Birmingham New Street in Railfreight livery while on a passenger working. This loco would end its days at Springs Branch depot, Wigan, in June 1999.

No. 31128, 4 August 1984

No. 31128 (D5546) rests between duties at Saltley depot, Birmingham, carrying BR blue livery. This loco is still in use today with Nemesis Rail, based at Burton upon Trent, having formerly been used by Fragonset Railways. No. 31128 is named *Charybdis*.

No. 31128, 15 November 2008

No. 31128 (D5546) sits inside the roundhouse at Barrow Hill while undergoing refurbishment for Nemesis Rail. The loco is seen having its Fragonset livery replaced by a coat of BR blue livery. No. 31128 carries the name *Charybdis*.

No. 31130, 23 August 2009

No. 31130 (D5548) runs round its train on the Battlefield Railway. This loco carries Railfreight Coal livery, and it also carried the name *Calder Hall Power Station*. There were not that many Class 31s named during the BR era, compared to other classes.

No. 31134, 25 June 1985

No. 31134 (D5552) is seen stabling at Saltley depot, Birmingham. This is one of the members of the class that doesn't carry a headcode box, only the discs, hence their nickname skinheads. No. 31134 was another Class 31 to end its days at Springs Branch depot, Wigan, being cut in July 1999 by EWS.

No. 31135, 1 June 1987

No. 31135 (D5553) stands at Saltley depot, Birmingham, waiting its next turn of duty. This Class 31 was unique in having the yellow window surrounds, this livery normally applied to other classes. This Class 31 was sold to T. J. Thomson, Stockton, for scrap, it being cut in January 2000.

No. 31141, 2 February 1985

No. 31141 (D5559) is seen stabled at Saltley depot, Birmingham, in BR blue livery. This skinhead would be withdrawn in 1989, and would be sold to M. C. Metals, Springburn, for scrap, and would be scrapped in Glasgow in October 1989.

No. 31141, 19 March 1987

No. 31141 (D5559) approaches Water Orton with a short Freightliner working. M. C. Metals, Springburn, would scrap No. 31141 two years later.

No. 31142, 1 June 1996

No. 31142 (D5560) runs through Crewe station with an overhead line maintenance train. These trains were converted from passenger-carrying MK1 carriages, and included a cable drum carrier, which can be seen behind the loco. No. 31142 was scrapped by T. J. Thomson, Stockton, in December 2003.

No. 31142, 30 August 1996

No. 31142 (D5560) stands alongside Carlisle Citadel station carrying Civil Engineers 'Dutch' livery. A Travelling Post Office (TPO) rake can be seen behind the loco. No. 31142 was withdrawn and then scrapped by T. J. Thomson, Stockton, in December 2003.

No. 31143, 22 February 1986

No. 31143 (D5561) rests at Saltley depot, Birmingham. This loco is seen carrying original Railfreight livery, which was applied to members of the class from 1985 onwards. Booth Roe Metals would scrap No. 31143 in August 1989.

No. 31144, 8 July 1996

No. 31144 (D5562) carries original Railfreight livery as it passes Saltley depot, Birmingham, with a scrap steel train. This had been released from Doncaster Works following overhaul a couple of months earlier. This loco survived for years at a private site in Manchester before being scrapped in 2012, although the cabs do survive.

No. 31144, 11 June 1986.

No. 31144 (D5562) awaits departure from Lawley Street Freightliner Terminal while carrying original Railfreight livery.

No. 31146, 17 June 1986

No. 31146 (D5564) shunts at Lawley Street Freightliner Terminal, Birmingham, before departure. This had not long been overhauled at Doncaster Works, during which it received a headlight and a repaint into original Railfreight livery. This would later be named *Brush Veteran*, and would be withdrawn with fire damage before being scrapped by Booth Roe Metals in July 2004.

No. 31159, 1 March 1991

No. 31159 (D5577) approaches Birmingham New Street with a coal working. No. 31159 would be withdrawn following collision damage in 1996, and would be sold to M. C. Metals, Springburn, for scrapping, which took place in June 1996.

No. 31159, 3 October 1985

No. 31159 (D5577) sits at Saltley in original Railfreight livery waiting its next turn of duty. This livery was certainly a change from the BR blue livery.

No. 31160, 24 November 1996

No. 31160 (D5578) sits forlornly in the snow at Wigan Springs Branch. This loco was withdrawn and awaiting scrapping, which took place in June 1999 by EWS. When delivered in 1960, this loco carried an experimental version of electric blue livery, but this would later be removed in favour of BR green. It would also carry the unofficial name *Phoenix*, which was applied by Tinsley depot.

No. 31163, 23 July 1998

No. 31163 (D5581) shunts out of the RMC sleeper factory at Washwood Heath, Birmingham, coupled to classmate No. 31110. Both locos carry Civil Engineers 'Dutch' livery. This loco was happily preserved and can be found at the Chinnor & Princes Risborough Railway.

No. 31164, 5 March 1986

No. 31164 (D5582) runs light engine past Saltley depot, Birmingham, carrying freshly applied original Railfreight livery. No. 31164 would be scrapped by T. J. Thomson, Stockton, in 2000.

No. 31175, 16 March 1985

No. 31175 (D5595) sits at Saltley depot, Birmingham, complete with a pair of Class 20 locos. This loco was unusual in that it carried its running number in the front headcode box. It would eventually be scrapped on site at Carlisle Kingmoor in 1988.

No. 31183, 29 May 1980

No. 31183 (D5604) is seen resting at Saltley depot, Birmingham, having been recently repainted into standard BR blue livery. No. 31183 would receive collision damage in 1988, and would be moved to Booth Roe Metals, Rotherham, for final scrapping in 1989.

No. 31188, 27 May 1980

No. 31188 (D5611) passes the gasholders at Washwood Heath with a steel working. This loco was preserved at the Wensleydale Railway, only to end up being sold to T. J. Thomson, Stockton, for scrap in 2008.

No. 31190, 4 May 2012

No. 31190 (D5613) is seen resting at Bescot in early 2012. No. 31190 has been repainted back into BR green livery, and is currently operated by British American Railway Services (BAR). This loco had originally been used by Fragonset following withdrawal from EWS.

No. 31190, 29 January 2013

No. 31190 (D5613) sits at Derby station while carrying a version of the BR green livery. This is one of the few Class 31s still able to run on the main line, and also carries its former number, D5613, on the secondman's cab side.

No. 31199, 19 March 1988

No. 31199 (D5623) rests at Tyseley depot, Birmingham, awaiting repairs along with classmate No. 31243. No. 31199 would be scrapped by T. J. Thomson, Stockton, in December 2003.

No. 31200, 21 May 2000

No. 31200 (D5624) sits condemned at Crewe South Yard. No. 31200 still carries Railfreight Coal livery, which was applied to certain members of the class that were based at Crewe. This loco would be sold to Harry Needle, and was moved to Carnforth, before being moved onto Throckmorton Airfield. It was then sold onto Network Rail, but it wasn't refurbished and instead it was stripped for spares until it was sold to C. F. Booth, Rotherham, for final scrapping, which occurred in 2007.

No. 31202, 24 August 1983

No. 31202 (D5626) trundles through Doncaster station with a bullion train, which consisted of three wagons and a carriage for the police guards. No. 31202 would have a spectacular end, falling onto the North Circular Road, North London, with classmate No. 31226 dropping on the top of it and breaking No. 31202 in half. The loco was cut in half where it stood before being sent to Vic Berry's for scrapping, which took place in 1989.

No. 31214, 31 July 1982

No. 31214 (D5638) is seen at Birmingham New Street with a rake of MK1 coaches. 31214 would have an early demise, being involved in a collision at Hope in May 1983, and would be moved to Doncaster Works for scrapping, which took place in October 1983.

No. 31215, 28 July 1984

No. 31215 (D5639) sits in the sun outside Tinsley depot, Sheffield. This loco was unique in the fact that it received collision damage repairs at Stratford, which resulted in it losing the headcode box at one end, but still retaining it at the other end. It would retain this unusual feature right until it was scrapped, which was in May 1995 at M. C. Metals, Springburn.

No. 31217, 23 August 1986

No. 31217 (D5642) rests at Saltley depot, Birmingham, carrying recently applied original Railfreight livery. This loco would end up as part of the Crewe-allocated Railfreight Coal liveried members, but would be scrapped by Vic Berry at their new premises near St Mary's Mill Lock in 1999.

No. 31219, 1 January 1997

No. 31219 (D5644) spends New Year's Day 1997 dumped in the withdrawn road at Toton Yard. The loco carries Civil Engineers 'Dutch' livery, and would be sold along with the other locos stored in this line to T. J. Thomson, Stockton, for scrapping, which took place in June 2003.

No. 31219, 24 February 1987

No. 31219 (D5644) is seen on the main Up line at Peterborough station with an OHLE Electrification coach. This was about the time when the Class 91s were being introduced to the East Coast Main Line.

No. 31222, 9 March 1985

No. 31222 (D5648) spends the weekend stabled at Bescot along with a Class 25 and a Class 47. These sidings have now been replaced with a virtual ballast quarry.

No. 31222, 16 May 1987

No. 31222 (D5648) is seen stabled at Tyseley depot, Birmingham, surrounded by other locos, including No. 40013 and No. 40135. No. 31222 would eventually suffer fire damage in 1988, and would find its way to Vic Berry's, Leicester, for scrapping, which took place in February 1990.

No. 31226, 6 July 1985

No. 31226 (D5652) passes Saltley depot, Birmingham, with a passenger working while carrying original Railfreight livery. This loco would end up on the roof of No. 31202 after the locos ran away from Cricklewood Yard, and ended up falling onto the North Circular Road, North London. Whereas No. 31202 was moved to Vic Berry's straight away, No. 31226 would spend a couple of years stored at Stratford, before being sent to M. C. Metals, Springburn, for final scrapping, which took place in October 1991.

No. 31229, 22 March 1981

No. 31229 (D5655) sits at Cambridge station at the head of a rake of MK2 carriages while carrying BR blue livery. This loco would be sold onto European Metal Recycling, Kingsbury, for scrapping, which finally took place in August 2001.

No. 31233, 28 May 1998

No. 31233 (D5660) powers through Stafford station, along with classmate No. 31203, with an engineers working. No. 31233 carried the name *Severn Valley Railway* at the time, and would go on to work for Network Rail on their measurement trains, and would be painted Network Rail yellow.

No. 31233, 8 March 2004
No. 31233 (D5660) sits outside the Railway Technical Centre (RTC), Derby, carrying Network Rail yellow livery.

No. 31233, 23 April 1996
No. 31233 (D5660) rests in the sidings adjacent to Chester station with a rake of Civil Engineers wagons. No. 31233 carries the name *Severn Valley Railway*, and unusually also carries Regional Railways branding underneath the nameplate.

No. 31235, 26 February 1988

No. 31235 (D5662) passes Washwood Heath light engine carrying red-stripe Railfreight livery. No. 31235 would go on to be preserved at the Mid Norfolk Railway.

No. 31237, 5 September 1992

No. 31237 (D5664) leads four classmates light engine through Washwood Heath as part of a light-engine convoy. No. 31237 carries Civil Engineers 'Dutch' livery, while the four classmates all carry original Railfreight livery. No. 31237 would end up stored at Toton, and would join many of its classmates at the time in being sent to T. J. Thomson, Stockton, for scrapping, which took place in September 2004.

No. 31238, 24 February 1987

No. 31238 (D5665) passes through Peterborough station with a rake of Civil Engineers wagons. No. 31238 carries recently applied red-stripe Railfreight livery, and would be scrapped at Wigan Springs Branch by EWS in August 1999.

No. 31243, 10 July 1993

No. 31243 (D5671) sits condemned at Stratford TMD, London in the summer of 1993. At this time there were quite a few withdrawn Class 31s to be found at Stratford, and they were mostly scrapped where they stood, No. 31243 being dispatched in February 1994.

No. 31243, 21 June 1989

No. 31243 (D5671) is seen stabled at Bescot TMD carrying original Railfreight livery. This loco would be scrapped at Stratford TMD, London, in February 1994.

No. 31243, 22 August 1986

No. 31243 (D5671) trundles light engine through Leeds station carrying original Railfreight livery.

No. 31244, 4 April 1980

No. 31244 (D5672) is seen resting at Saltley depot, Birmingham. Note the tablet catcher recess in the cab door, a design that wasn't carried by many members of the class, and still carried unusually as late as 1980. This was another Class 31 to be withdrawn early following collision damage, which occurred in September 1982, and was cut up at Doncaster Works in September 1983.

No. 31247, 10 July 1994

No. 31247 (D5675) sits at Toton depot, Nottingham, carrying red-stripe Railfreight livery. At this time, this was allocated to the weekend only use pool, and would eventually be stored at Toton before being sent to T. J. Thomson, Stockton, for scrapping, which occurred in June 2003.

No. 31248, 24 July 1990

No. 31248 (D5676) arrives at Derby station with a passenger working, which consisted of four Network South East liveried MK2 carriages. No. 31248 was eventually sold to T. J. Thomson, Stockton, for scrap, and final cutting took place in March 2000.

No. 31255, 4 July 1985

No. 31255 (D5683) arrives at Lawley Street container terminal, Saltley, light engine. At this time almost any class of loco could turn up to work these services, from Class 25s to Class 58s. No. 31255 was chosen by EWS to receive a trial version of the EWS maroon-and-gold livery, and in this livery it would be preserved at the Colne Valley Railway.

No. 31257, 1 August 1987

No. 31257 (D5685) works through Bescot station with a Civil Engineers working, while still carrying BR blue livery. This loco would be scrapped by Booth Roe Metals, Rotherham, in April 1992.

No. 31261, 26 July 1986

No. 31261 (D5689) leads fellow classmate No. 31102 past Saltley depot with a rake of MK1 carriages, heading for Birmingham New Street. Both locos carry original Railfreight livery. No. 31261 would only last in service until the end of the year, being involved in a collision with No. 31245 in December 1986, and would be scrapped at Stratford TMD in 1988.

No. 31262, 4 September 1982

No. 31262 (D5690) is seen ready to depart from Birmingham New Street with a working to Cambridge. No. 31262 would be another early withdrawal, again following collision damage, which it received in May 1983, and would be scrapped at Doncaster Works in July 1983.

No. 31270, 26 October 1993

No. 31270 (D5800) arrives at Crewe station with a short Civil Engineers working, which consisted of just two wagons. The loco carries a headlight on the cab front, and also a set of miniature snowploughs, which improved the look of the loco. It also carries Railfreight coal markings. No. 31270 would go on to be preserved, and can be found at Peak Rail, Matlock.

No. 31271, 7 April 2002

No. 31271 (D5801) is seen preserved at the Midland Railway Centre, Butterley. The loco carries Railfreight construction livery, and is seen on a set of recently repainted bogies.

No. 31271, 30 July 1992

No. 31271 (D5801) departs Washwood Heath with a rake of brand new sleepers from the nearby RMC sleeper factory. The loco carries Railfreight construction livery.

No. 31273, 4 April 1985

No. 31273 (D5803) rests at Saltley depot, Birmingham, in BR blue livery. This loco carries miniature snowploughs. This loco would eventually be scrapped by Booth Roe Metals, Rotherham in May 2004.

No. 31275, 2 September 1995

No. 31275 (D5805) is seen stabled adjacent to Carlisle station. No. 31275 carries Railfreight coal livery, and also carries the Crewe depot symbol of the Cheshire cat on the secondman's cab side. This loco was withdrawn following derailment damage it received at Carnforth in 1997, and would be scrapped on site at Carnforth in February 2005.

No. 31276, 2 June 1991

No. 31276 (D5806) is seen stabled at Saltley depot, Birmingham, carrying Railfreight coal livery, and is complete with a Crewe depot plaque. No. 31276 also carries the name *Calder Hall Power Station*, which would be removed when it was transferred to Immingham, and the plaques were then fitted to No. 31130. No. 31276 was sold to T. J. Thomson, Stockton, for scrap, and it was finally cut in February 2000.

No. 31277, 13 September 1985

No. 31277 (D5807) is seen stabled at Saltley depot, Birmingham. This loco was allocated to Thornaby depot at the time, and they have added their own livery embellishments, being a white stripe just under the roof, a red buffer beam and a Kingfisher depot symbol. No. 31277 would later be chosen to be rebuilt as an ETH-fitted example, being renumbered No. 31469 in 1987. It would later have the equipment isolated, and would be further renumbered to No. 31569. As No. 31569 it would be sold to T. J. Thomson for scrap, which was completed in June 2003.

No. 31278, 29 May 1988

No. 31278 (D5808) ticks over at its home depot of Thornaby. This was another Class 31 to receive a local alteration to the livery, gaining Thornaby-style large numbers. No. 31278 would last less than twelve more months in service, being withdrawn in March 1989. It would be scrapped by December 1989 by M. C. Metals, Springburn.

No. 31281, 3 May 1988

No. 31281 (D5811) stands at Gateshead depot, Newcastle. Again, another Thornaby addition to the livery includes large numbers and a Kingfisher logo on the middle of the body side. This loco would be withdrawn in May 1989, and was sent to Vic Berry, Leicester, for scrapping, which they completed in February 1990.

No. 31281, 22 February 1976

No. 31281 (D5811) is seen at Immingham depot just a couple of years after gaining its TOPS number. No. 31281 would be scrapped by Vic Berry, Leicester, in February 1990.

No. 31282, 29 May 1988

No. 31282 (D5813) is seen stabled at Thornaby depot, carrying red-stripe Railfreight livery. Of note is the Thornaby Kingfisher depot sticker just behind the cab door. No. 31282 would eventually be scrapped at European Metal Recycling, Kingsbury, in December 2001.

No. 31285, 18 March 2013
No. 31285 (D5817) approaches Water Orton carrying Network Rail yellow livery while hauling a test train.

No. 31289, 24 March 1991
No. 31289 (D5821) stands at Saltley depot, Birmingham, in BR blue livery. This loco was finally sold to Fragonset for further use in 1999. It was then preserved at the Northampton & Lamport Railway, before finally being moved to the Rushden Transport Museum.

No. 31293, 10 July 1993

No. 31293 (D5826) is seen at Stratford depot, London, having been withdrawn nearly three years earlier. At this time Stratford was the home to quite a few withdrawn Class 31 locos, and they would be scrapped where they stood. No. 31293 would be scrapped in February 1994.

No. 31296 29 September 1987

No. 31296 (D5829) is seen at Saltley depot, Birmingham, in original Railfreight livery. No. 31296 also carries the name *Tren Nwyddau Amlwch*, but on the other side of the loco the name read *Amlwch Freighter*. This loco was eventually withdrawn in December 1993, but it would be another ten years before it would be scrapped, which took place at L&NWR, Crewe, in January 2004.

No. 31301, 7 June 2009

No. 31301 (D5834) is seen at MOD Long Martston in long-term secure storage. Underneath all the rust, the loco carries red-stripe Railfreight livery, and was withdrawn back in 1998. It was originally sold to Fragonset Railways for refurbishment, though this was not forthcoming, and was then sold onto Nemesis Rail who decided to send it for scrap, this being done by C. F. Booth, Rotherham, in February 2011.

No. 31304, 19 August 1982

No. 31304 (D5837) departs Lawley Street Freightliner Terminal with a loaded container working. The loco carries the standard BR blue livery, and was withdrawn in 1996. It was moved to Springs Branch depot, Wigan, for component recovery, and would finally be scrapped in July 1999.

No. 31304, 24 February 1987

No. 31304 (D5837) runs through the centre road at Peterborough with a rake of mineral wagons. The loco shows signs of refurbishment, being fitted with a headlight and also having been repainted into original Railfreight livery. This loco would be scrapped at Springs Branch depot, Wigan, in July 1999.

No. 31305, 26 December 1991

No. 31305 (D5838) sits condemned at Bescot depot, Walsall. The loco stands in front of the old steam shed, which has recently been demolished. The loco would stay at Bescot for another three years before being sold to M. C. Metals, Springburn, who would scrap the loco in June 1994.

No. 31309, 1 June 1987

No. 31309 (D5843) is seen at Saltley depot, Birmingham, while acting as bank engine. These locos were required to bank heavy freights up the Camp Hill line towards Bordseley. No. 31309 carries the name *Cricklewood*, which it had received two weeks before. The loco also carries a white stripe, larger than normal numbers, and also a red buffer beam, which improved the appearance greatly. No. 31309 would be withdrawn in 1991 and would be sold to Booth Roe Metals, Rotherham, for scrap, which was completed at the end of April 1992.

No. 31312, 20 November 1994

No. 31312 (D5846) sits at Springs Branch depot, Wigan. The loco carries Railfreight Coal markings, from when it had been allocated to Crewe. The loco would remain in service until March 1996, when it was stored. The loco would be scrapped on site at Wigan in November 1999.

No. 31319, 30 May 1993

No. 31319 (D5853) is seen at Shrewsbury station while coupled with No. 31130. Both locos were shuttling between Shrewsbury and Hereford, as the two yards had an open day at the same time. Both locos carry Railfreight Coal markings. No. 31319 would be stored in 1998, and would then be sold to Harry Needle Railroad Company, and would be moved to Carnforth for storage before being sold to Network Rail as a source of spares for their small Class 31 fleet. It would later be sold to C. F. Booth, Rotherham, for scrap, which they completed in June 2007.

No. 31323, 5 July 1986

No. 31323 (D5858) is seen stabled at Saltley depot, Birmingham, carrying BR blue livery. Being a Thornaby allocated loco, it would receive a white stripe and also a Kingfisher depot symbol on the bodyside. No. 31323 would be withdrawn in June 1989 following fire damage, and would be sold to M. C. Metals, Springburn, for scrap, which they completed in September 1991.

No. 31324, 22 April 1987

No. 31324 (D5859) passes through Nuneaton station with a rake of Civil Engineers ballast wagons. No. 31324 would lead an uneventful life, being transferred around various Eastern region sheds before being withdrawn from Crewe in 1993. It would then be sold to Booth Roe Metals, Rotherham, for scrap, and was cut up in May 1994.

No. 31327, 1 March 1981

No. 31327 (D5862) stands at Doncaster station with a rake of Civil Engineers ballast wagons. This was the last Class 31 to be built, being completed at the end of 1962. This loco would later be named *Phillips-Imperial*, and would happily go on to be preserved, and can be found at the Strathspey Railway, Aviemore.

No. 31327, 6 May 1974

No. 31327 (D5862) passes through Derby station with a Civil Engineers ballast working. If the headcode is correct, it is running as 6M25. This loco had only been renumbered with its TOPS number four months previously, and would go on to be preserved at the Strathspey Railway, Aviemore.

No. 31327, 24 May 1987

No. 31327 (D5862) is seen inside the shed at Thornaby depot. The loco has its newly applied nameplate, *Phillips-Imperial*, covered in readiness for its naming ceremony the following day, which took place at Port Clarence, Teesside.

No. 31401, 18 August 1982

No. 31401 (D5589) is seen departing Bristol Temple Meads station coupled with No. 31420 on a passenger working. 31401 would be condemned with collision damage in March 1988, and would be scrapped at Doncaster Works in September 1988.

No. 31403, 27 May 1996

No. 31403 (D5596) sits forlornly at Toton Yard having been stored for a couple of months. It would later be withdrawn in September 1996, before being sold on to T. J. Thomson, Stockton, for scrap. It would sit at Toton for another four years before moving north to be scrapped, which was completed by June 2003. Of note is the position of the ETH jumper cable to the right of the right-hand buffer, when originally fitted it was positioned just under the right-hand side foothold.

No. 31404, 22 October 1984

No. 31404 (D5605) is seen passing Saltley depot, Birmingham, complete with a Finsbury Park added white stripe. The initial batch of Class 31/4s was allocated to Finsbury Park, London, for East Coast passenger workings out of Kings Cross, and quite a few received the white stripe similar to No. 31404. This loco would be withdrawn in 1991, and was sold to Booth Roe Metals, Rotherham, who would scrap the loco in March 1994.

No. 31405, 3 October 1985

No. 31405 (D5606) rests at Saltley depot, Birmingham. Just visible are the remains of the white stripe this loco would have carried when it was allocated to Finsbury Park in the late 1970s. No. 31405 would later be named *Mappa Mundi* when it was allocated to Bescot, and would be scrapped at Doncaster Wood Yard in April 2000.

No. 31408, 24 August 1984

No. 31408 (D5646) stands at Leeds station with a rake of MK1 carriages. This would probably have been a Trans Pennine working towards Manchester, the Class 31/4s taking over these duties from Class 123 and Class 124 DMUs. No. 31408 would end up being scrapped at Springs Branch depot, Wigan, in March 2001.

No. 31411, 29 December 1984

No. 31411 (D5691) rests at Saltley depot, Birmingham, in between Christmas and New Year 1984. No. 31411 still carries the white stripe it received while allocated to Finsbury Park, and unusually it also carries its running number on both cab sides, not just on the driver's side. No. 31411 would end up being sold to Fragonset Railways, and was stored at Barrow Hill from 2002 onwards. However, it would be sold to Ron Hull Junior, Rotherham, for scrap and this would be completed in November 2005.

No. 31415, 13 April 1980

No. 31415 (D5824) rests on one of the turntable roads at its home depot of Old Oak Common, London. This shot proves that not only Finsbury Park allocated Class 31/4s received the white stripe, but also some of the Old Oak Common allocated members received it as well. 31415 would later be sold to Fragonset Railways and later onto Nemesis Rail, before finally being sent to C. F. Booth, Rotherham, for scrap, which was completed in July 2009.

No. 31416, 19 July 1986

No. 31416 (D5842) passes Saltley depot, Birmingham, along with classmate No. 31424 with the 10.50 working from Yarmouth to Birmingham New Street. No. 31416 carries a Stratford-style silver roof, which it carried along with No. 31412, after working a special Ford Executive charter train for a month in 1985. No. 31416 would have its ETH equipment isolated in 1990, and would be renumbered No. 31516. In this guise it would be withdrawn, and would be sold to Harry Needle Railroad Company, who sent it to European Metal Recycling, Kingsbury, for scrapping, which would take place in October 2001.

No. 31416, 17 March 1983

No. 31416 (D5842) arrives light engine at Birmingham New Street, backing onto a passenger working, ready to head back towards East Anglia. No. 31416 carries a white stripe it would have received when allocated to Old Oak Common depot, London, but it has had a replacement cab door at the far end, as the stripe doesn't extend over the door. European Metal Recycling, Kingsbury, would scrap No. 31416 in October 2001.

No. 31417, 5 April 1987

No. 31417 (D5856) is seen at rest at Saltley depot, Birmingham, carrying standard BR blue livery, albeit a little work stained. This would be another Class 31/4 that would end up being stored at Barrow Hill, but was eventually sold to Ron Hull Junior, Rotherham, for scrap, which was completed in December 2005.

No. 31417, 16 February 1984

No. 31417 (D5856) passes Saltley depot, Birmingham, at the head of a rake of London Underground tube stock. No. 31417 would eventually be scrapped by Ron Hull Junior, Rotherham, in December 2005.

No. 31417, 16 October 2005

No. 31417 (D5856) stands forlornly at Barrow Hill awaiting a decision on its future. It would only sit at Barrow Hill for another two weeks, being sent to Ron Hull Junior, Rotherham, for scrap, which was completed just over two months later.

No. 31418, 20 September 2009

No. 31418 (D5522) is seen inside the main restoration shed at the Midland Railway Centre, Butterley, while undergoing a complete restoration. No. 31418 should have been renumbered No. 31104 when it received its TOPS number, however it was fitted with ETH equipment and became No. 31418 instead, and is the only member of the initial batch of ETH Class 31/4s to be rebuilt from a skinhead example.

No. 31418, 24 February 1987

No. 31418 (D5522) is seen making a station call at Peterborough station while on a passenger working. Of note is the running number on the front, an unusual addition for the time. No. 31418 would happily be preserved at the Midland Railway Centre, Butterley.

No. 31420, 25 February 1993

No. 31420 (D5591) passes through Crewe station with an ECS move consisting of an MK3 DVT and an MK2 TSO. No. 31420 was rebuilt from No. 31172 in 1974, when it was fitted with ETH equipment and renumbered at the same time. In this view it carries InterCity Mainline livery, which was only applied to a handful of the class. No. 31420 would end up being used to test the ETH equipment and to preheat carriages stabled at Old Oak Common, performing this duty until 2004. Unfortunately it would be sent to C. F. Booth, Rotherham, for scrap in July 2007.

No. 31421, 20 October 1996

No. 31421 (D5558) is seen stabled at Crewe depot carrying Regional Railways livery. This had been named *Wigan Pier*, but the plates had been removed. A handful of the class received this livery for use on passenger workings in the Manchester area, before being replaced by DMUs. No. 31421 was rebuilt from No. 31140 in 1974, and was initially preserved at the Midland Railway Centre, Butterley, but unfortunately it was sold for scrap to European Metal Recycling, Kingsbury, who scrapped it in August 2007.

No. 31422, 21 July 1984

No. 31422 (D5844) passes Saltley depot, Birmingham, with a summer Saturday working from East Anglia towards Birmingham New Street along with classmate No. 31423. These services would eventually be changed to a Stratford-based Class 47. No. 31422 was rebuilt from No. 31310 in 1974 when it had ETH equipment fitted. This loco would eventually receive InterCity Mainline livery. It would be sent for scrap to C. F. Booth, Rotherham, which was completed in October 2014.

No. 31422, 20 May 1996

No. 31422 (D5844) is seen in InterCity Mainline livery paired with No. 31465, which carries Regional Railways livery. They are seen at Chester station while engaged on Civil Engineers ballast work, which probably originated from Penmaenmawr. C. F. Booth would scrap No. 31422 in October 2014, having been stored at Tyseley depot, Birmingham, for many years.

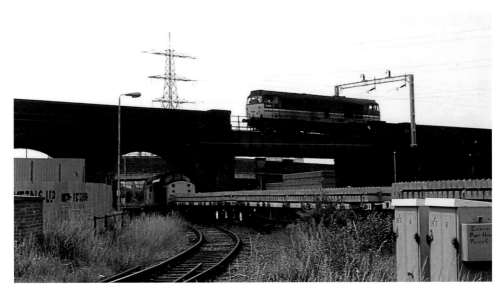

No. 31422, 23 July 1996

No. 31422 (D5844) passes over Washwood Heath, Birmingham, on the Aston to Stechford line, while underneath is the main line from Birmingham New Street to Derby. No. 37519 shunts sleeper wagons as the Class 31 goes overhead. The line in the foreground is the line into the old Metro Cammell factory, which is now the home of BAR, British American Railway Services. No. 31422 would end up being scrapped by C. F. Booth, Rotherham, in October 2014.

No. 31423, 7 June 2009

No. 31423 (D5621) is seen in derelict condition in long-term secure storage at Long Marston. Underneath the coat of blue paint, it carries the remains of InterCity Mainline livery. No. 31423 was rebuilt from No. 31197 in 1975, when it had its ETH equipment fitted. It would also receive the name *Jerome K. Jerome*. After withdrawal, this was sold to Fragonset Railways before arriving at Long Marston. It would eventually be sold to T. J. Thomson, Stockton, for scrap, which took place in October 2009.

No. 31425, 2 June 1987

No. 31425 (D5804) is seen at Lawley Street Freightliner Terminal, Birmingham. No. 31425 was rebuilt from No. 31274 in 1983, and was the first of an extra batch of Class 31s that was fitted with ETH equipment and renumbered. No. 31425 carries Network South East branding, an unusual feature. No. 31425 would eventually be withdrawn in December 1991, and would be sold for scrap to Booth Roe Metals, Rotherham, who completed the job in June 1994.

No. 31426, 11 December 1985

No. 31426 (D5617) rests at Saltley depot, Birmingham, with a couple of Class 47s. No. 31426 was rebuilt from No. 31193 in 1983. This loco would have its ETH equipment isolated in 1990, and would be renumbered No. 31526. In this guise it would be withdrawn and then sold to Fragonset Railways, who renumbered it back to No. 31426. It would eventually find its way to Ron Hull Junior, Rotherham, for scrap, and it would be dispatched in November 2006.

No. 31428, 10 August 1988

No. 31428 (D5635) is seen stabled in the old parcels bay at Leeds station. This area has now been redeveloped and contains extra platforms. No. 31428 was renumbered from No. 31211 in 1983 and carries the name *The North Yorkshire Moors Railway*, although the plates would be removed and refitted to No. 31439 after No. 31428 received fire damage, which resulted in its withdrawal, in 1991. It was then sold to Harry Needle Railroad Company who moved it to European Metal Recycling, Kingsbury, who scrapped it in December 2001.

No. 31429, 27 March 1993

No. 31429 (D5699) is seen dumped at Crewe depot, having been withdrawn in December 1991. No. 31429 was rebuilt from No. 31269 in 1983, and would be sold to Booth Roe Metals, Rotherham, for scrap, and it would meet its end in May 1994.

No. 31430, 9 October 1988

No. 31430 (D5695) stands at Bescot depot, Walsall, not long after it had been named *Sister Dora*. It had received a few local embellishments for the ceremony, namely a grey roof, silver buffers, cast builder's plate, cast steam-age depot plaque on the cab front and cast numbers. No. 31430 was rebuilt from 31265 in 1983, would go on to have its ETH equipment isolated and was further renumbered No. 31530. Happily this would go on to be preserved at the Mid Norfolk Railway.

No. 31434, 23 April 1996

No. 31434 (D5686) trundles light engine through Manchester Victoria hauling No. 37087. No. 31434 was rebuilt from No. 31258 in 1984 and would lead an uneventful life before being stored at Healey Mills. It was then sold on to Booth Roe Metals, Rotherham, for scrap, and was duly dealt with in April 2003.

No. 31439, 5 August 1996

No. 31439 (D5666) is seen at Washwood Heath along with classmate No. 31105. No. 31439 carries the name *The North Yorkshire Moors Railway*, and received the plates from withdrawn classmate No. 31428. No. 31439 was rebuilt from No. 31239 in 1984, and is seen carrying Regional Railways livery. It would later be sold to Fragonset Railways, who then sold it to Nemesis Rail, who sent it to C. F. Booth, Rotherham, for scrapping, which took place in March 2011.

No. 31439, 7 June 2009

No. 31439 (D5666) is seen in long-term secure storage at MOD Long Marston. A coat of blue paint to try and prevent rust has nearly covered its Regional Railways livery. No. 31439 was rebuilt from No. 31239 in 1984 at Doncaster Works, in which it gained ETH equipment. Unfortunately it would end up going from Long Marston to C. F. Booth, Rotherham, for scrap, this taking place in March 2011.

No. 31442, 27 March 1993

No. 31442 (D5679) waits departure time from platform 12 at Crewe with a rake of Regional Railways liveried MK2 carriages. No. 31442 was rebuilt from No. 31251 in 1984, and this view shows the roof detail to good effect. No. 31442 would eventually be withdrawn and stored at the Railway Age, Crewe, pending sale to the Churnet Valley Railway for preservation. The move never materialised, and the loco was instead sold to Booth Roe Metals, Rotherham, for scrap, which happened in September 2004.

No. 31442, 31 May 2000

No. 31442 (D5679) is seen in storage at the Railway Age, Crewe. This was rebuilt from No. 31251 in 1984, and it was sold to Booth Roe Metals, Rotherham, for scrap. It would be cut up in September 2004.

No. 31443, 8 March 1986

No. 31443 (D5598) stands at Tyseley depot, Birmingham, along with other various locos. This loco was rebuilt from No. 31177 in 1984, and would only last five years in service, being withdrawn following fire damage. It would be sold to Vic Berry, Leicester, for scrapping, which was completed in June 1990.

No. 31447, 28 July 1984

No. 31447 (D5828) is seen at Doncaster Works open day in 1984, having just been rebuilt from 31295, and had yet to be released to traffic. It would later have its ETH equipment isolated, and was renumbered No. 31547. It was later sold to T. J. Thomson for scrap, which occurred in November 2002.

No. 31449, 6 May 1985

No. 31449 (D5840) hurries past Saltley depot, Birmingham, with a passenger working. This was rebuilt from No. 31307 in 1984, and would lead an uneventful life until withdrawal in 1996. However, during this time its ETH equipment was isolated, and it was renumbered No. 31549. It would be sold to Fragonset Railways and moved to Tyseley Museum for secure storage. Unfortunately it would not be refurbished, and was sent to Ron Hull Junior, Rotherham, for scrap, which occurred in February 2005.

No. 31450, 6 April 1987

No. 31450 (D5551) stands at Saltley depot, Birmingham, waiting its next turn of duty. This was rebuilt from No. 31133 in 1984, and this was one of just a handful of skinhead Class 31s converted to a Class 31/4. This was finally withdrawn in December 1998 before being dispatched to Springs Branch depot, Wigan, for component recovery and final scrapping that occurred in May 1999.

No. 31450, 20 October 1996

No. 31450 (D5551) is seen under repair at Crewe depot. Rebuilt from No. 31133 in 1984, it would head to Springs Branch depot, Wigan, for final scrapping, which was completed in May 1999.

No. 31452, 8 September 2000

No. 31452 (D5809) is seen stabled at Saltley depot, Birmingham, in Fragonset Railways livery. This was rebuilt from No. 31279 in 1984 at Doncaster Works, and would eventually have its ETH equipment isolated and would be renumbered No. 31552. The loco carries the name *Minotaur*, which was applied by Fragonset. This loco is still in use on the main line today, and can be seen on spot hire duty.

No. 31452, 11 April 2007

No. 31452 (D5809) passes Washwood Heath towing Anglia liveried No. 47714 and some MK3 FO carriages towards Tyseley. No. 31452 carries the name *Minotaur*, and carries Fragonset black livery. It was rebuilt from No. 31279 at Doncaster Works in 1984, and would go on to have its ETH equipment isolated and be renumbered No. 31552, before reverting to No. 31452 under Fragonset.

No. 31452, 30 August 1998

No. 31452 (D5809) is seen at Toton depot open day 1998, having just been released from Tyseley Museum following refurbishment and repainting into Fragonset livery. This loco is still running on the main line today, carrying green livery.

No. 31454, 19 March 1988

No. 31454 (D5654) is seen stabled outside Tyseley depot, Birmingham, in a very poor external state. No. 31454 was rebuilt from No. 31228 in 1984, and would go on to be renumbered No. 31554 when it had its ETH equipment isolated. It would later be sold to Fragonset Railways, who refurbished it and repainted it into InterCity Mainline livery. This loco still survives today, based at the Weardale Railway working for British American Railway Services.

No. 31455, 2 September 1995

No. 31455 (D5674) stands adjacent to Carlisle station. Rebuilt from No. 31246 in 1984 at Doncaster Works, this loco would eventually find itself working from Crewe and being painted in Regional Railways livery, as seen in the photograph. It had once carried the name *Our Eli*, but this had been removed a couple of months earlier. This would be another Class 31 that would end its days at Springs Branch depot, Wigan, being scrapped there in February 2000.

No. 31455, 6 August 1989

No. 31455 (D5674) rests at Saltley depot, Birmingham, having not long been released from works overhaul, and carries a newly applied livery of departmental grey. Not the most inspiring of liveries, many that wore this livery later gained a yellow stripe along the top, which was then known as Civil Engineers 'Dutch' livery. No. 31455 was rebuilt from No. 31246 at Doncaster Works in 1984, and would last for another ten years, before being scrapped by EWS at Springs Branch depot, Wigan, in February 2000.

No. 31459, 2 August 2007

No. 31459 (D5684) stands outside its birthplace, Brush Loughborough. The loco was rebuilt from No. 31256 at Doncaster Works in 1984, and is seen carrying the name *Cerberus*. It gained this name when it was overhauled by Fragonset Railways, and also carries a version of their livery, being black, but without the maroon stripe. This loco still survives today, based at the RTC, Derby, working for RVEL.

No. 31459, 16 July 2000

No. 31459 (D5684) is seen at Tyseley Museum during the final stages of its overhaul by Fragonset Railways, who had brought the loco from EWS. The loco carries Fragonset Railways livery, and also the name *Cerberus*. No. 31459 was rebuilt from No. 31256 in 1984 at Doncaster Works and still survives today, being based at the RTC, Derby, working for RVEL.

No. 31459, 29 September 1998

No. 31459 (D5684) sits forlornly in the yard at Tyseley Museum having been brought by Fragonset Railways for further use. Despite the condition, the loco was fully refurbished, emerging from Tyseley nearly two years later wearing Fragonset livery and the name *Cerberus*. No. 31459 was rebuilt from No. 31256 at Doncaster Works in 1984.

No. 31461, 18 August 1988

No. 31461 (D5547) powers south through Northallerton with a mixed bag of parcel vans. No. 31461 was rebuilt from No. 31129 at Doncaster Works in 1985, and was one of only three rebuilt from skinhead examples, No. 31444 and No. 31450 being the other two. This was another Class 31/4 to be sold to Fragonset Railways, moving to Tyseley for evaluation in 1998. The overhaul was not forthcoming, however it is now owned by Nemesis Rail and can be found today at Burton upon Trent.

No. 31461, 28 March 1987

No. 31461 (D5547) rests at Tyseley depot, Birmingham, along with classmate No. 31407. No. 31461 was rebuilt from No. 31129 at Doncaster Works in 1985, and would go on to be sold to Fragonset Railways for refurbishment in the late 1990s. The overhaul would not happen, but the loco survives today, being based at Burton upon Trent under the ownership of Nemesis Rail.

No. 31462, 17 July 2005

No. 31462 (D5849) is seen stabled on one of the turntable roads at Tyseley Museum, having been sold to Fragonset Railways. No. 31462 was rebuilt from No. 31315 at Doncaster Works in 1985, and would lead an uneventful life until withdrawal in 1998. Fragonset moved the loco to Tyseley for possible overhaul, but the loco was stripped of spare parts before being sent to Ron Hull Junior, Rotherham, for scrap in 2006.

No. 31464, 25 September 1987

No. 31464 (D5860) rests at Saltley carrying standard BR blue livery. This loco was rebuilt from No. 31325 at Doncaster Works in 1985, but would lead only a short life of five years in service as a Class 31/4, suffering collision damage in 1990 at Allerton. The collision damage resulted in it being condemned, and it was scrapped at M. C. Metals, Springburn, in 1991.

No. 31465, 6 August 2000

No. 31465 (D5637) stands dumped at Old Oak Common during the open day of 2000. This loco was rebuilt from No. 31213 in 1985 at Doncaster Works and would end up allocated to Crewe for Regional Railways passenger workings, and it is seen in that livery. It would be stored at Old Oak Common for many years before being sold to Network Rail for use on their test trains, and has recently been sold by Network Rail to Harry Needle for further use.

No. 31465, 22 April 1996

No. 31465 (D5637) arrives at the sidings adjacent to Chester station with a rake of Regional Railways liveried MK2 carriages. The loco was rebuilt from No. 31213 at Doncaster Works in 1985, and can be seen carrying Regional Railways livery to match the coaching stock. This loco would be brought by Network Rail for use on their test trains, and has only recently been withdrawn by them, and sold to Harry Needle for further use.

No. 31466, 3 July 1996

No. 31466 (D5533) works north through Peterborough station with a rake of Civil Engineers ballast wagons. This loco was rebuilt from 31115 at Doncaster Works in 1985, and would lead an uneventful life first working passenger trains, then being relegated to ballast workings, including a repaint into Civil Engineers 'Dutch' livery. In 1998 it would be chosen to be repainted into EWS livery, the only member of the class to be treated, except for No. 31255, which was only used for test purposes. The loco was preserved, and is based on the East Lancashire Railway.

No. 31466, 30 August 1996

No. 31466 (D5533) is seen on display at the EWS open day at Toton in 1998. This was the only member of the class to receive EWS livery, although 31255 was used for test purposes. No. 31466 was rebuilt from No. 31115 at Doncaster Works in 1985, and is currently preserved in this livery at the East Lancashire Railway.

No. 31466, 31 March 1986

No. 31466 (D5533) rests at Saltley depot, Birmingham, along with classmates No. 31162 and No. 31441. No. 31466 was rebuilt from No. 31115 at Doncaster Works in 1985, and survived long enough to be preserved at the East Lancashire Railway.

No. 31467, 23 May 1996

No. 31467 (D5641) is seen stabled at Chester station with a rake of Civil Engineers ballast wagons, coupled with classmate No. 31421. No. 31467 was rebuilt from No. 31216 at Doncaster Works in 1985, and would carry BR standard blue livery right through to withdrawal. It was preserved by the East Lancashire Railway, but was another unfortunate member to be scrapped, this being completed by European Metal Recycling, Kingsbury, in August 2008.

No. 31468, 15 July 1996

No. 31468 (D5855) departs the RMC sleeper factory with a rake of brand new sleepers along with classmate No. 31545. No. 31468 was rebuilt from No. 31321, and was initially the last to be rebuilt at Doncaster in 1985. No. 31468 carries the name *The Engineman's Fund*, and also wears Civil Engineers 'Dutch' livery. It would later have its ETH equipment isolated and be renumbered No. 31568. This loco would go on to be sold to Fragonset Railways who refurbished the loco for main line use, and also named it *Hydra*. It would eventually be sold to British American Railway Services, and it is based at the Weardale Railway.

No. 31514, 24 November 1996

No. 31514 (D5814) sits in the snow at Springs Branch depot, Wigan. This loco was renumbered from No. 31414 when its ETH equipment was isolated in 1990, and also carries Civil Engineers 'Dutch' livery. It would happily be preserved at the Ecclesbourne Valley Railway.

No. 31516, 2 January 1992

No. 31516 (D5842) passes through Crewe station with an ECS working, which includes MK2 and MK3 carriages and an MK3 DVT. The loco was renumbered from No. 31416 when its ETH equipment was isolated in 1990, and also carries Civil Engineers 'Dutch' livery. It would be withdrawn in 1998, and would be sent to European Metal Recycling, Kingsbury, for scrap, which was completed in October 2001.

No. 31516, 3 December 1995

No. 31516 (D5842) sits dumped at Cardiff Canton in 1995. It had been out of use for a few months, but would not be officially withdrawn until 1998. 31516 was renumbered from No. 31416 in 1990 when its ETH equipment was isolated, and would be sold to European Metal Recycling, Kingsbury, for scrap, and it was cut up in October 2001.

No. 31524, 16 October 2005

No. 31524 (D5575) stands forlornly at Barrow Hill awaiting a decision on its future. This loco was originally numbered No. 31157, but when it was selected to have ETH equipment fitted in January 1975 it became No. 31424. The equipment would later be isolated, and it became No. 31524, as seen here. It was stored in 1996, and would eventually be sold to Fragonset Railways, who moved it to Barrow Hill for storage, pending possible refurbishment. Unfortunately it was sold to Ron Hull Junior, Rotherham, for scrap, which was duly completed in August 2006.

No. 31544, 26 June 1993

No. 31544 (D5555) trundles light engine through Doncaster station carrying Civil Engineers 'Dutch' livery. No. 31544 was originally numbered No. 31137. This was one of only three skinhead Class 31s to be converted, No. 31129 and No. 31133 being the others. When the ETH equipment on No. 31444 was isolated, it became No. 31544 as shown. It also carries the name *Keighley & Worth Valley Railway*, which it received in 1988. This would be another member of the class to end up at Springs Branch depot, Wigan, for component recovery and final scrapping, which took place in March 2001.

No. 31545, 2 April 1993

No. 31545 (D5833) rests at Saltley depot, Birmingham, carrying work-stained standard BR blue livery. This loco was originally numbered No. 31300 before being rebuilt as an ETH-fitted member of the class, and became No. 31445. It would last six years as a Class 31/4, before the ETH equipment was isolated and it became No. 31545. It would be stored in 1997 before being sold to Booth Roe Metals, Rotherham, for scrap, which they completed in October 2002.

No. 31548, 26 December 2000

No. 31548 (D5566) is seen condemned at Bescot depot. This loco was originally numbered No. 31148 before being rebuilt at Doncaster Works and emerging as No. 31448. Later on the ETH equipment would be isolated, and it was renumbered No. 31548. It was stored as early as 1995, and sat at Bescot for nearly six years, before being sold to Harry Needle Railroad Company, who sent it to European Metal Recycling, Kingsbury, for scrap, which was completed in June 2001.

No. 31558, 17 July 2005

No. 31558 (D5836) sits withdrawn on one of the turntable roads at Tyseley Railway Museum, having been stripped of spare parts, and also having the cab side number panel removed. This loco was rebuilt at Doncaster Works from No. 31303, becoming No. 31458 after the fitting of ETH equipment. As with all other Class 31/5s, the equipment was isolated, resulting in its renumbering to No. 31558. In this guise it was named *Nene Valley Railway*, but the plates were removed in 1997. It was initially sold to Harry Needle for scrap, but instead it was resold to Fragonset Railways, who stored it at Tyseley. Another class member that was not to be refurbished, it was sold to Ron Hull Junior, Rotherham, being scrapped in December 2005.

No. 31568, 6 May 1990

No. 31568 (D5855) is seen at Bescot open day, 1990, having just been named *The Engineman's Fund*. The loco carries plain departmental grey livery, however it would later receive a yellow stripe, becoming Civil Engineers 'Dutch' liveried. This was originally numbered No. 31321, before being rebuilt as No. 31468 at Doncaster Works in 1985. When the ETH equipment was isolated, it became No. 31568 as seen. This loco was later sold to Fragonset Railways, who refurbished the loco, naming it *Hydra*, and put it back in traffic as No. 31468. The loco is still around today, and is based at the Weardale Railway.

No. 31601, 2 August 2007

No. 31601 (D5609) stands at Derby carrying Wessex Trains livery. This loco was numbered No. 31186, and lead an uneventful life until withdrawal in 1996. It was sold to Fragonset Railways who refurbished the loco at Tyseley, and fitted ETH equipment, renumbering it No. 31601. It was hired to Wessex Trains for passenger workings, hence the pink livery, and is seen carrying the name *Gauge O Guild*. The loco can still be seen on the main line today, operated by British American Railway Services, but carries Devon & Cornwall livery.

No. 31601, 21 May 2000

No. 31601 (D5609) stands on display at the Adtranz Crewe Works open day in 2000. The loco carries Fragonset livery, and the name *Bletchley Park Station X*. This was refurbished by Fragonset at Tyseley in 1998, being renumbered from No. 31186 as a result of having ETH equipment fitted.

No. 31970, 3 May 1990

No. 31970 (D5861) stands at Derby station carrying RTC red and white livery. This loco was originally numbered No. 31326, and was the penultimate member of the class to be built. It was withdrawn from general use in 1987, before being allocated to Derby RTC for departmental work. It was renumbered No. 97204, in line with other RTC locos. However, it was later renumbered No. 31970. It would last just over a year in this guise, being withdrawn in December 1990 with a defective engine. It was stored at Crewe Works, before being scrapped there in March 1997.

No. 97203, 1 August 1987

No. 97203 (D5831) sits condemned at Bescot depot, Walsall. This loco was originally numbered No. 31298, before being withdrawn from service in 1986, when it was then allocated to the RTC, Derby. It was renumbered No. 97203, repainted into RTC house colours and was used on test trains. It would only last for nine months in this guise following fire damage on a test train. It would be written off, and No. 31326 was converted to No. 97204 to replace No. 97203. It would be sold to Booth Roe Metals for scrap, which was completed in December 1989.

No. ADB968013, 15 May 1983

No. ADB968013 (D5513) sits condemned at Doncaster Works in 1983. This Class 31 was originally numbered No. 31013, and was withdrawn from operating stock in 1979, having spent all its life allocated to Stratford depot, London. It was then taken into departmental stock as a carriage-heating loco, being based at Great Yarmouth and Cambridge, and was one of four such locos used for these purposes. Scrapping was completed in July 1983. The loco carries BR green livery.

No. ADB968014, 25 February 1984

No. ADB968014 (D5502) is seen inside the melt shop at Crewe Works waiting for final scrapping. This was renumbered from No. 31002, and was one of four original series Class 31s that were converted to carriage-heating locos based on the Eastern Region. It would only carry out these duties for two years, being finally withdrawn in October 1982, and it would be sent to Crewe Works for scrapping which was completed three months after the photograph was taken.

No. ADB968015, 15 May 1983

No. ADB968015 (D5514) stands condemned at Doncaster Works. This was withdrawn from Stratford depot in 1976 as No. 31014, and was selected to become a carriage-heating loco based on the Eastern Region. It was renumbered No. ADB968015, and would provide heating duties until being stored in October 1982. It was later sent to Doncaster Works for scrap, and this was duly completed in June 1983, just one month after this photograph was taken.

No. ADB968016, 27 October 1984

No. ADB968016 (D5508) stands withdrawn on the Crewe Works scrap line. This loco was taken out of service at Stratford in 1980, and was one of four original Class 31s to be converted to carriage-heating locos on the Eastern Region. Renumbered from 31008, and only lasting two years before final withdrawal, it was sent to Crewe Works for scrapping, which was completed in June 1985, being the final member of the quartet to be scrapped.

No. 31018, 30 August 1998

No. 31018 (D5500) is seen on display at Toton open day, 1998. This was the first Class 31 to be built at Brush, Loughborough, being released to traffic in October 1957. It would only last in service for nineteen years, being withdrawn in 1976, but was saved for preservation by the National Railway Museum, York.

No. 31103, 3 September 1967

No. 31103 (D5521) rests at Saltley depot, Birmingham. At the time this Class 31 was allocated to Ipswich. It would be renumbered No. 31103 in 1974, and would be withdrawn from operating stock in 1980. It would be sent to Swindon Works for scrap, this being completed in February 1983.

No. 31162, 7 April 2002

No. 31162 (5580) is seen preserved at the Midland Railway Centre, Butterley. This loco lead a fairly uneventful life until withdrawal from Immingham depot in 1992. It would be sold to the A1A group for preservation, and was based at Butterley.

No. 31230, 20 August 1967

No. 31230 (D5657) is seen in BR green livery under the coal stage at Saltley depot, Birmingham. Emerging from Brush, Loughborough, in 1960, this loco would spend thirty-four years in service before being stored in 1994. It would later be sold to T. J. Thomson, Stockton, for scrap, which was completed in March 2000.

No. 31442, 27 May 1967

No. 31442 (D5679) works through Derby station along with classmate No. 31144 (D5562) with a rake of ESSO two-axle oil tanks. By strange coincidence, both locos would enter preservation, only for both to be subsequently scrapped. 31442 would be scrapped by C. F. Booth, Rotherham, in September 2004.

No. 31563, 2 August 2007

No. 31563 (D5830) is seen preserved at the Great Central Railway. This loco was originally numbered No. 31297, and was another to enter the ETH rebuild programme at Doncaster, emerging as No. 31463 in February 1985. Later on it would have the ETH equipment isolated and was renumbered No. 31563, and was withdrawn from service in 1996. It was then sold to the Great Central Railway, and it is seen wearing a version of the Bronze Gold livery worn as an experiment by No. 31400 (D5579) when it was built.

No. 31311, 11 October 1967

No. 31311 (D5845) awaits departure from Sheffield Midland. D5845 would be renumbered No. 31311 in 1974, and would last in service until 1989, when it was withdrawn from Toton depot. It would be sent to M. C. Metals, Springburn, for scrap, which they completed in December 1989.

No. 31327, 17 September 2015

No. 31327 (D5862) is seen preserved at the Strathspey Railway, Aviemore. This was the last Class 31 to be built, emerging from Brush, Loughborough, in October 1962. This would be an Eastern Region loco for all its life, until moving to Crewe in 1993.